LONELY DAYS – FOUNDATION

In life we all need a foundation

Foundations that are solid

Pure

Clean

Void of instability

Sin

Pressure

Stress

We need foundations that have natural beauty – serenity

The natural beauty of the world void of smog

Harmful chemicals

Toxins that pollute the air we breathe

Life is guaranteed but within the framework of life humans came

They devoured

Destroy the beauty of life for self gain

So called self preservation

We became hungry

Angry

Sinful

Thoughtless

Polluted

Vile

We are no longer children of beauty

We are no longer natural

We've become hated

Hatred

Hate

The beauty of earth is no longer within us

It's gone

Irreplaceable

Destroyed by greed

Anger

Self hate

Self pity

Sin

Death

Self Preservation

And as we cry, we fail to see our failings

Fail to build lasting and solid foundations

Homes

Pyramids

We fail to see God – Good God

Build solid and lasting foundations with God – Good God

We fail to do all hence our (human) foundations are built on lies

Deceit

Anger

Stress and pain

Greed

Michelle Jean

Foundations are built to last

They are more solid than rocks

They are rich in history

Culture

Heritage

Pride

Good foundations are the key to life

They are not stepping stones

Nor are they flawed

In life God – Good God is our good foundation

Our lifeline

Good hope

Charity

True love

Finding him is rare but he is there

He's just a phone call away

He is the foundation of life

We just have to build him in truth

Good thought

Prayer

We are his children and he is our rock and mountain – framework

Good life and goodness

He is our good all, hence we have to build with him and make all we do in him last forever ever.

Michelle Jean

We are the pyramids of life

We grow

Sometimes erode

Die

We are the framework of life

Its foundation

The leaf of life

Tree of life

Beautiful garden

Eden

And although we fade

We continue to grow

Grow up in goodness if you are good

But grow down in death if you are evil

The foundation of life does not start with me and you

It starts with God – Good God

Planted in our genes

DNA

We are life because life was given to us in the form of water

Friction

Heat

Vibration

Sight

Vision

Thought

Earth

Dirt

Energy

All these we need because in all we see and do, we are a part of the foundation of life – good life, spiritual life – the universe.

Michelle Jean

The pathway to life is your gateway to heaven

It's your light

Your tree

Your garden of hope

Lifeline

In all that you do, you need to live good and clean

You must be honest and true then you will see paradise

The true Garden of Eden which is you

You are the light and the way

The foundation of God – Good God

You are his hope for a better today

Tomorrow

You are his sanctuary

His home

House

Rose garden

You are is present

His future

Universe

You are his lifeline

Dateline

Time

Gateway and pathway

Hence set good and solid foundations so that you can truly live with him.

See him

Partake of him

Truly be with him

Michelle Jean

In all that I see and read I have to question; go to him Good God in thought with my feelings, doubts, truths – everything.

Yes life is a given but there are many questions pertaining to life that we do not know.

Some say they don't believe in God and we came out of a bang – huge bang in time. So the questions I ask is, how did atoms come into being – collide if someone did not make the framework and or foundations for these atoms to collide?

How did water come about if atoms collided?

How do you explain snow – cold weather?

How do you explain physical and spiritual nature – foliage?

Plants and animals

You

Do you not need water – fluids – semen for the framework of you? So how can you base you on an accident, collision if there was a foundation and framework for you – DNA?

The heat of atoms is far greater than the heat of the sun because all is done in time – spiritual time and man knows not, nor hath the key to this time – realm. So how can you (man – humanity) base anything off collision when man – humanity knows not the scope of NOTHING IN TIME? In time (your time) YOUR NOTHING IS SOMETHING HENCE NOTHING IS SOMETHING AND SOMETHING IS NOTHING WHICH IS SOMETHING.

Michelle Jean

As humans what we do not know we cast aside as nonsense – fiction. We do not think hence we say there is no God.

But if there was no God, there would be no atom.

If there was no God, there would be no you.

If there was no God, there would be no heat nor would there be fire.

There would be no friction and vibration if there was no God.

God is the framework hence all in the universe known and unknown to man – humanity he created.

How he God – Good God came into being is another story hence the true origins and birth of life humanity do not know. I know not this true origin hence God – Good God is unknown to man – humanity.

Know this, if atoms collide and or there was a big bang you nor I and this earth and universe would exist because like I've said, the fires of man is not the fires of atoms – the atomic world.

Hence foundations and framework was laid out for everything known and unknown to man – humanity.

Michelle Jean

Now I go back to your time, hence the bible (book humans read and call holy); that which is called the book of sin in the spiritual world – realm.

Good God I have to go there because in all of the foundations and ground work and framework humanity has and have of you, built and say it is of you is wrong – not true. The framework and foundation humans have of you has and have eroded; hath no good and or solid framework and foundation.

As I go back to the book of Genesis and look into the framework of Adam, I have to come to you because something here is so not right.

Man said Eve was made and or formed from the rib of Adam. You took a rib from Adam to make Eve.

Yes I know better because that rib was Adam's sperm hence Adam was Eve's Father and Lover – husband. Hence the nastiness and lies of man but that is not why I came here.

I came here because like I said, something is not right on the part of Adam because Adam was lonely and you gave him a help mate from himself that was not good nor was she clean. Hence Adam was mother, father, sister, brother and what have you to Eve. ADAM WAS NOT CLEAN HENCE HE BROUGHT FORTH AN UNCLEAN – DIRTY CHILD AND WIFE, HENCE THEY HAD DIRTY – UNCLEAN CHILDREN.

*Eve was asexually produced then because no female gene he (Adam and or you) required to produce his own child and wife. Yes people can poke holes in this but I am going to leave things as is. **Adam did not require nor did you require a woman to produce Eve. SO EVE DID NOT COME FROM A FEMALE SHE CAME FROM A MALE AS PER THE BOOK OF SIN – MAN'S HOLY BIBLE.**_

SO MAN – MALES DO NOT HAVE ANY GROUNDS AND OR FOUNDATION TO LAY AND OR THROW THEIR LIES AND GUILT ON WHEN IT COMES TO WOMAN AND SIN.

SIN DID NOT COME FROM A WOMAN, IT CAME FROM A MAN HENCE ADAM WAS THE FATHER AND HUSBAND OF SIN. HE GAVE BIRTH TO SIN BECAUSE SIN CAME FROM HIM IN THE FORM OF EVE. **NO FEMALE GENE WAS REQUIRED AND NO FEMALE GENE WAS USED.**

*The book of sin did not say you made a woman and gave her to Adam. The book of sin specifically said, you took a **rib not sperm from Adam and made woman Eve.** So, no man on the face of the planet can blame females – woman for sin when sin came from man – males without the function, union, foundation and framework of a female. Hence males are the true sinners of this world and universe not females.*

Now the question I ask you Good God is, if Adam was so pure and good, of good creation sorry of formation, why did Eve come bad? (This taken from the perception of the book of sin, man's holy bible).

I mean in the garden there was no sin right?

So if you took a rib from Adam to make Eve (Evening) then Eve should have been good and true to you?

She could not have sinned if you made all that was good and true – pure? So something is so not right with the Adam and Eve saga – story.

I more than infinitely and indefinitely know that good cannot turn to evil because he or she is made good and the foundation of goodness cannot erode nor can it be broken down.

Erosion is not a part of the framework and foundation of good life.

*Death is not a part of the framework and foundation of good life hence the Adam and Eve story in the Garden of Eden does not fly nor does it wash with me. This story is a lie **hence the bible's framework and foundation is based on lies and deceit – stories and or tales that are not true.***

Like I've told you before Good God, I need our foundation and now framework of life and goodness to be more than infinitely and indefinitely and more than forever ever solid and true – good. Our framework and foundation cannot erode or be broken down by me or anyone or anything including time and weather. Our framework must stand for more than infinite and indefinite lifetimes and generations to come in truth and goodness, honesty and purity – the truth of all good life forever more including all that is good and true in the universe and beyond.

This is what I need with you and from you indefinitely so when the book of sin tells me you do not build good foundations, I turn that around now and say, sin does not build good and true foundations. I know for a fact that sin kill, destroy and breakdown. So in all that sin writes in their holy bible – book of sin, I know it is truly not you Good God.

Your foundation and framework cannot fate or rot hence we are to know you; know your goodness and truth.

Truth cannot fade

Goodness cannot fade

Good life cannot fade

Hence all you build and create cannot be of evil, it must be of goodness and truth.

Tell me something, can goodness give anything that is bad?

No it cannot right?

So why then would we as humans – humanity think that you created and give bad things when you are good and can only create and give goodness – good things?

Yes negative energy is there hence the different poles – the pull of the north from the south.

North – the North Pole pulls people to it including land and lands – water.

Hence the North is heavy

Heavy burdened, sinful

Warring

Hated, hatred and hate

Overly populated

In disarray

In all negative energy do and does, it takes all from the south and amass greater land and lands, Resources, more people, more water, more food and universe – power – negative energy.

North cannot stand to see the south prosper hence the north say 9/10th and giveth only 1/10th to good; that which is you Good God.

So 9/10th belongs to the North and 1/10th belongs to the South; hence the Circle and or Whole of life in the eyes of man and Satan – evil beings and or negative energy.

Michelle Jean

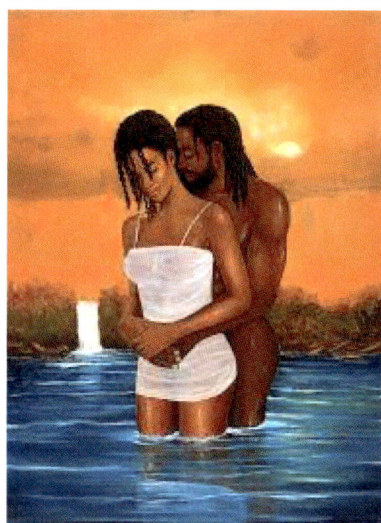

These pictures I own them not. They were taken from Google Images to prove a point. If all came into being with a big bang none of this (the scenery from the pictures above including animal and human life) would not exist. We are beauty but as humans we cannot see the beauty in things nor can we see beauty in each other.

We are the ones to destroy nature.
We are the ones to destroy all that is good around us.
We are the ones to destroy life and that's truly a pity.

Michelle Jean

In all that I've tried in my life I've failed

In all that I've tried to do for me and my family I've failed

Prayers go up

Answers seldom return.

I am lost now

Without hope

Given up

The will is not there to continue

Hence I must leave life alone

This isn't a test for me

But a battle of spiritual and physical will

I have to give up because I have no fight left in me.

I cannot build

Nor can I continue to hold on to someone or something that have not my best interest at heart.

I cannot play the fool anymore hence I must go my own way and truly leave him (Good God) alone.

Michelle Jean

I cannot see my own life

Fate anymore

I cannot rely on an entity that sees my pain and do nothing to truly help me

Ease my hurt – burdened heart.

I am but woman but I feel the pain of life

I feel the pain of motherhood

Childbirth

Raising my children alone

I cannot go anymore

I cannot do anymore

Hence I have to abandon ship

Too much water coming in on me

Too much stress and pain

I cry out

The spirit cries out

But I am left alone to face hardships and pain

There is no help from the black race above hence I am left alone time and time again

I am left to fend for self

Left for dead

I cannot rely on my God for my financial security hence I must truly leave him because one day I am up but for the rest of the days, months and years I am truly down.

I truly see no hope in him because I look to the future and doubt him in respect to saving his own.

If he can let me suffer financially like this, then what say he for the future of his children – people?

This non help has to stop hence on many of my journeys in the spiritual realm I was left to fend for myself by my own black men – black race.

There was no help from them. I had to help myself hence I fully comprehend why Black People do not help black people in both realms.

Yes I was told why too because in all that we do, we have no good will towards each other.

So as it is in the spiritual realm, so it is in the physical realm.

Women were to fend for self.

Feel pain and heartache because men, a lot of men are non factors. They truly don't care for and or about their own. So as they do not care, as women we have to care and raise our own (children) by our self.

We have to do what it takes to raise our children by our self.

We have to stay strong and bare the burden no matter how stressful it gets.

We have to do it all because all is left on us to do by these men women.

Good God is no exception because in the spiritual realm he's a male and he's left me to do all for him by myself. Yes you can say this is trust but this isn't trust to me but heartache and pain.

Like you I need my life to be fulfilled

Completed

Happy

Truly peaceful

Joyful

But this cannot be because I cannot find peace within.

Every corner I turn I am shut down.

Every move I want and need to make I cannot.

Every road I take it's the wrong road.

So where do I turn if God – Good God himself have no conclusive direction for me to take – go?

He too is leaving me in limbo hence I have to turn and let go of him.

A happy relationship you stay in, but an unhappy relationship you truly leave alone because it brings you stress and heartache – lots of pain.

Hence I tell you I would never tell you to choose and or chose my god because I know the pain I feel, the pain I have to endure. I will however tell you TO LIVE YOUR LIFE CLEAN AND IN GOODNESS AND TRUTH BECAUSE AT THE END OF

THE DAY, NO GOD IS WORTH IT IF YOU ARE LIVING YOUR LIFE IN PAIN AND DISARRAY – HEARTACHE.

Like I've said, the truth cannot hurt and if a god knows your trials and tribulations, heartaches and pain and just stand aside and look without truly helping you out of the situation you are in, then he and or she is truly not worth it. They too are contributing to your heartache and pain – sorrows.

They too are contributing to your sins. Hence they did not truly love you.

There is only so much heartache and pain the spirit can go through before it snaps to pieces. Hence I wonder about my god, the one that I choose time and time again.

Yes he said to write but what good is writing when no one is reading what you are writing?

What good is writing when he's imprisoning you?

What good is writing when you are shackled and chained?

Hence what good is asking when you truly cannot receive?

What good is truth in the living when you have to cheat your way to get this or that?

What good is truth when you have to stray from it?

What good is truth when you have to beg your own god for it (truth) – goodness – good food?

What good is God – Good God if he truly cannot give?

What good is God – Good God when he cannot relieve your heartache and pain right away?

What good is God – Good God when he cannot truly answer you properly?

What good is God – Good God if he can't build properly and we as humans can breakdown and tear down not only his framework and foundations but our framework and foundations?

Yes evil provides for his own right away because evil does not want his people to stray. He gives them their wants right away but with Good God you have to beg whilst he keeps you crying and waiting and this is truly not fair to us as human beings.

Yes these are my lonely days

My confusing days

Doubtful days

Eroding foundations and framework

Yes these are my depressing days because I cannot do my own good will for self. So because I am not happy, I have to truly look into my life and see if this god is whom and what I want and need.

I've spent so many years truly loving him and now I think it was all for naught – in vain. I cannot continue living a lonely and depressing life hence I truly have to do for me all around.

True love is not one way and in all your giving, if all you get is heartache and pain then that person and or god is truly not worth it. You are sinning self and truly loving the wrong person and or god.

Lies are cheap but they are believable hence many of us fall prey to lies.

We are hurt by lies.

We die by lies

Marry in lies

Commit to lies

Death

I can no longer do this for my god hence a vacation is now out of the question. I have to put aside all that hurts me including the god I truly love.

You cannot give truth and true love and get naught in return.

You cannot put your life on hold for someone and in return they abandon you and say you are breaking them down. So what good were you to that person in the first place?

If you have a solid foundation that foundation will last for thousands of years no matter the storms, different weather it faces.

That foundation cannot erode because that foundation was well built – more than solid.

So because I do not have a solid and impenetrable foundation with Good God, I now have to leave him alone in truth because he is truly not good for me. HIS FOUNDATION IS NOT SOLID ENOUGH FOR ME. IT IS TOO WEAK HENCE HE

CANNOT BE MY TRUE STRENGTH IN TIMES OF NEED – TROUBLES – FINANCIAL HARDSHIPS AND PAIN.

For me, when you give, give to last so that that person cannot be broken down again.

Give so that person can truly be stress free.

Give so that that person can truly help themselves for the better in the long run – future.

Give so that that person do not have to run to you time and time again for help.

We were not born beggars but in all that I find, we have to turn to begging because he Good God made it so.

We are like dogs begging at his table even though he says we are his children – seeds. As humans we do lose faith and hope and God – Good God has not learnt this over the ages; hence we leave him because his road is too damned hard and filled with pain – shackles and chains.

His way should not be hard.

The way to evil should be hard come on now.

Life – good life is given but yet good life can be broken because of trust issues.

Foundations that are built on goodness and truth, trust cannot be broken in the living nor can it be broken in death – the death of flesh.

These foundations are so solid that they are forever ever because they were built in goodness and in truth. Goodness and honesty prevailed hence truth cannot die it can only live forever ever.

If we have not trust for God – Good God and the foundations and framework he's laid out for us what good is he to us?

If we cannot trust him with our lives then what good is he (Good God) to us?

If we cannot trust him with our future then what good is he (Good God) to us?

Yes good life was given but where is the trust?

Yes as humans we fail you but if all that we've been give is mistrust and lies, then we will mistrust you and lie to you and on you. And this is what we as humans have and has done over the centuries.

You cannot mistrust or distrust goodness because goodness is good, but we do anyway because of what we were taught – learned.

IF THE BOOK OF MAN IS WRONG GOOD GOD, THEN IN TRUE TRUTH, YOU WILL BE WRONG ALSO. So as the book of man (holy bible) is wrong then you are wrong also because man say the writers of the bible were divinely inspired and of you. So if this is so and the holy bible to man is true, then you are a liar because death, rape murder, stealing and destruction is in the bible – man's book of lies and deceit and they did say it was from you. So you give lies according to man hence you are a liar just like man and you cannot be trusted nor are you true according to man and the book of man and not of you. As humans we made you wrong hence all that you have done for us is truly wrong. And if all that you have truly done for is truly wrong then we can never ever be right – just – clean.

Michelle Jean

Yes it's the last day of April 2014 and I have to write this book no matter how small it is.

On this day there are no happy days for me but financial stress.

I know it is said, seek and ye shall find but what good are you if you seek and you cannot find?

What good are you if all you do you get shot down in different directions?

What good are you in your search if each and every time you search you get massive headaches?

What good are you in your search if you do not know the direction to search in and when you are told a direction to go in you fail miserably?

Hence trust is also key to life and if you cannot trust the god you praise and serve what good is either of you to each other?

If you cannot trust him to take you and or truly help you out of your financial predicament, health woes and troubles, heartache and pain, then he's no good to you nor is he right for you.

YOU CANNOT TRULY LOVE AND HAVE NOT TRUST. YOU MUST HAVE TRUST IN TRUTH AND IF YOU DO NOT HAVE TRUST THEN YOU HAVE NOT TRUTH.

There must be truth in true love and there are no ands ifs or buts about this.

One cannot love true and the other love, it will not work.

True love is unconditional and without restrictions and boundaries. If there are boundaries then something is truly wrong.

Freedom hath no boundaries in a free and good world – society.

To have boundaries means you are restricted – controlled. It's not to say you are to take unclean things in your world. You cannot, you must stay clean and true. You must have truth – good integrity.

Foundations are laid yes but if those foundations can be broken what good are they to anyone like I've said?

God – Good God cannot build foundations that can be broken hence I have to question his strength and his creations.

I have to question him because in my world with him, there are no weaknesses there are only absolute truth and honesty – trust. I do not need weak anything because weaknesses are flaws. Hence if we are not stronger than anything on earth and in the universe even known and unknown to man and spirit, how can we have a perfect world and universe void of all sin and evil – wickedness, injustice and death.

I do not want sin and or any form of wickedness and evil in our new abode, so if he is not willing to build strong then sin will come back in. Sin will continue to reside with man and sin will continue to infiltrate our happy home and destroy it all.

He too have to take responsibility for his own actions. Like I've said time and time again, he cannot continue to sustain and maintain people that do not want or need him.

He cannot continue to sustain and maintain people that say he does not exist when they know for a fact he does.

He cannot continue to sustain and maintain people that say they believe but as soon as they turn their backs, they praise and worship sin – the devil in their so called homes – churches.

He cannot continue to bend over for death's children because death's children do not want or need him nor did they choose him. They tell lies on him and run him like he is of evil – the devil himself.

Death's children chose death hence death must now provide for his and her own.

It's not fair for to those who are trying to live clean and you Good God and earth continuously maintain and sustain wicked and evil people. It's as if you ignore your people and put evil and their children on pedestals – first.

As people trying to live clean and good we face a lot of hardships in life and that is not right nor is it fair to us.

We have to contend with sin and live amongst sin.

Some of us are killed daily by wicked and evil people – sin's children.

Some of us have to raise our children alone which is not easy when daddy is not around. Some men look down upon us – single moms like we have no worth. We are not married hence we are bad – punished for being a single parent. This is the reality of some of us because no one see's our hardships and grief. No one see our struggles, all they see is a single parent trying to make it on their own by doing the best they can with the little means that they have.

Some of us did not abandon our children; we kept going despite the hardships. Some of us do what we need to do to get by.

Some of these father's don't think hence many will not have a place in your abode. They abandoned their children and left them to suffer, hence I know our children are not guaranteed to get us into your abode Good God.

Good and strong foundations are key and if you do not have good and solid foundations in your family life then you have nothing and are nothing.

You cannot teach a child to do wrong and think it is good.

You cannot abandon a child and say you had to because the mother is such and such.

NO MOTHER CAN OR WILL STOP A GOOD MAN FROM SEEING HIS CHILD. COME ON NOW.

NO FATHER CAN OR WILL STOP A GOOD WOMAN FROM SEEING HER CHILD COME ON NOW.

We are the ones to teach wrong and when our children mess up we say they are bad – evil – wrong even demonic and sinful. As parents we forget about the problems we gave to our parents whilst growing up..

When we are disobedient we carry on the tradition of disobedience, hence goodness seldom comes. Meaning the problems we gave to our parents is returned unto you but greater. Meaning you will have more heartache and pain – stress. So truly look into you and the problems and or trouble you gave as a child growing up. Certain things you said to your parents as a child, your children and or one child will come and tell you the same words. This I know from experience because my children (one child) did tell me these same words.

Some fathers and mothers abandon their children and after the child have made it in life them come crawling back like dogs with their tail between their legs and play the "Honour thy father and thy mother that thy days be long" bullshit in front of their child.

KNOW THIS: FOR ALL YOU FATHERS AND MOTHERS THAT ABANDON YOUR CHILDREN AND OR CHILD AND USE THE HONOUR THY FATHER AND MOTHER BULLSHIT, THAT CHILD OWES YOU NOTHING AND THEY DO NOT HAVE TO HONOUR YOU BECAUSE YOU DID NOT RAISE THEM NOR DID YOU DO ANYTHING FOR THEM.

You left them (your children) hence they are not obligated to you. BY YOU ABANDONING THEM, YOU RELINQUISHED ALL RIGHTS TO THEM IN THE SIGHT OF MAN AND GOD – GOOD GOD.

You are no longer looked upon as a parent hence that child does not have to honour you nor does he or she have to help you in old age. They must however honour the person and or persons that raised them in goodness and truth. That person and or persons that raised them took on the role of Mother and Father. That person cannot change the child's birth certificate but that child can however honour them by adding her parent or parents last name to the birth certificate of his or her child and or children.

For example, your last name is Kingston.

That child can name his or her child Kingston John Anderson or John Frederick Kingston Anderson. By that child doing this they are acknowledging you and honouring you as a parent. To keep the legacy going that child must keep Kingston in the family tree from generation to generation because you are now a part of his and or her family. Your name is equally important as his or her last name. Hence it is wise to give your children good names AND NOT BABYLONIAN NAMES.

Yes you are to commission your child to do this and pass this tradition down from generation to generation. This means that child can save you AND MUST SAVE YOU because you treated him or her good. You instilled good in this child hence you are looked upon as parent – the parent of this child.

Do not look at genetics but look at you and the good that you do.

Remember and never forget this: YOU ARE THAT CHILD'S GOOD FOUNDATION HENCE BE STRONG AND CONTINUE TO MAKE YOUR FOUNDATION (BOND) WITH THAT CHILD SOLID, UNBREAKABLE AND UNSHAKEABLE – GOOD AND HONEST – TRUE AND CLEAN. Never teach that child to hate because if you do then you are taking away from your foundation with that child and Good God including the good universe.

Yes some people look at hue – skin colour but do not look upon hue and or skin colour because as the spirit sheds the flesh, it too must shed the hue of flesh. Know this and never forget it.

Once the hue is gone we have pure energy and this is where and or how change comes about.

Listen there is a better place for God's – Good God's children and you need to know this as well as hold on to this knowledge. You are his child and he has a good place waiting for you. All your troubles have nothing to do with him, it hath to do with man – other human beings that live to control and dominate – kill and you need to know this. All that is happening on earth hath nothing to do with Allelujah but man – wicked and evil people that live for greed – financial gain and financial slavery. To these people God – Good God does not exist but I am telling you, he Good God exists. Hell exist hence the death of wicked and evil people in the physical and spiritual world – realm. As the children of Good God he's been trying to save us and we need to listen and take heed because the death and slavery of humanity cometh globally and if you are not on board with Good God then you will be left behind and you will die. Good God is our saving grace so save yourself because better does come for the good and pure at heart. You know not the beauty of Good God and if I could show you his beauty and grace on earth I would. You cannot imagine his beauty because all the beauty of earth, humanity, this universe cannot compare to his true love and beauty – perfection. His good kingdom awaits you but you have to hold on and be clean. Live good and clean on earth because if you don't you will not get to him nor will you live in his house – home. His home awaits you but without your true foundation you cannot build with him nor can anyone build that foundation for you if they are not ordained to.

He Good God need a clean and good home hence YOU HAVE TO BE HIS GOOD, CLEAN AND TRUE HOME ON EARTH.

YOU HAVE TO BE HIS GOOD AND TRUE SAVING GRACE.

YOU HAVE TO BE HIS OBEDIENT CHILD AND OR CHILDREN THAT LISTEN TO HIM NO MATTER YOUR STRUGGLES AND PAIN ON EARTH AND IN THE SPIRITUAL REALM.

So please do right by him and you.

Always build good and strong foundations that will last from generation unto generation. Yes as good people we face a lot of trials and tribulations hence I get down on God – Good God about this. He too must learn that we hurt and feel pain and he cannot continue to neglect us.

He cannot continue to let others cause us pain nor can he permit others to hurt us and take our lives. This is not right hence the separation of Good and Evil must come. Good will always pass over death hence good cannot stay in the realm and realms of evil. Evil destroy and good replenishes – preserve all that is good and true in truth and honesty.

We say we are solid in him (God) but if we were truly solid in him the stresses of life would not reach us. Our lives would not be rocked by death, heartache, stress, pain, obeah, voodoo, health woes and financial pain – slavery.

All these things would not reach us. We would be stress free and solid in all that we do. So stand firm and stronger than a rock and cry to him with your truths.

Abide with him in all that you do and your trials and tribulations will go away – end. He will sort them out for you but give him time.

Abide with him in goodness and in truth and he will show you his magnificence.

Abide with him and death will pass you over because you are living good and clean – true with him.

Abide with him and by him and he will walk with you.

He will lift you up when you are down.

He will put a smile on your face when you need to ease your heartache.

When the devil say they are singing for him, you lift your hand to him (Good God) in thanks because you've found him and you don't want to share him nor do you want to let him go.

You will be lifted up to his glory because his victory is yours at all times.

When the enemies and enemy come to devour you with their lies, shame and deceit, he will show you them before they come so that you can pray and cry to him for victory. Trust me they will fall at the wayside this I know because I've made him (Good God) my strong and good foundation. I've made him my all no matter my tears because I know better days are yet to come for me and him.

Trust me if I could hold his hand and grab on to him and not let him go like a human I would.

I would look upon his glory and say thank you for choosing me and being with me. I would say to him, I am with you because you reside in me and I am a true gift and child of you. I would take his hand like a child taking their mother's or father's hand and say, truly thank you because you more than complete me in all that I do for thee.

I would clasp my hand and bow at his feet and say you are my Glory Allelujah and I more than truly thank you for good life, this earth, my earthly mother, you, my children, my family and the good and true seeds you gave me.

I would hug him like a lover truly in love and clasp my hand around his neck and say, you are my good all and truth and without you I am nothing.

I would take his hand and pull him to the dance floor and dance with him to I CAN ONLY IMAGINE BY TAMELA MANN. Yes we would rock to Beautiful by Romain Virgo because he is more than beautiful and wonderful to me even when I get tired.

So as I dedicate I CAN ONLY IMAGINE BY TAMELA MANN TO HIM GOOD GOD, I DEDICATE THIS SONG TO YOU ALSO. If you are going through trials and tribulations think of him Good God and play this song and think of how wonderful and beautiful Good God and his kingdom is.

Think of him as if you are standing before him in awe.

Better is yet to come and you will stand with him in his glory but only if you are good and clean.

People and family holy is he.

Glory, glory, glory is he and he's my glory and true peace of mind.

Trust me you don't know just how wonderful he is because if you did you would feel what I feel and the tears would come. You would smile and say I have him, I have my Glory Allelujah and I don't want to let him go for anyone and anything.

You would look to the day when your eyes truly behold him and touch him.

Trust me I need him and his foundation with me to be more solid than the Pyramids of life. Hence our upward triangle can never fade, lose colour, crumble, rust or be broken for more than infinite and indefinite lifetimes and generations.

To me, if I am broken he is broken and if he is broken then I am broken.

So in my book he must be stronger than life because he created life, making him life – good life all around.

In our new kingdom Satan shouldn't be able to come knocking at our door and doors.

Death should not come knocking either.

The children of sin and evil should not come knocking either. We should be infinitely and indefinitely separate from them at all times. Good hath nothing to do with evil hence evil should not have anything to do with life and good life. Nor should evil and wicked people be able to taunt and take good and true life – people no matter how hard they try.

Hence the foundation that I need Good God to now lay for his people should be inpenitrable like I've said. This time around sin should not be able to tempt his Good God's people because he Good God should ensure his foundation – good and true framework, foundation and people that truly loves him more than life itself should not come in contact with death's children and or anything that is unclean and evil – wicked.

We should be infinite and indefinite universes a part.

There's no testing because no one can test the truth nor can they test true love.

Can a man test God?

So why should man test good – good and true people when they know that person is good and true – live by the true, good, clean and honest integrity of Good God? Come on now.

Tell me something, would God – Good God give someone unclean meat to eat if he knows the meat is unclean – not good for them?

Would God – Good God sent you into the lion's den knowing that the lion would devour you?

Would God – Good God send you into places that are unclean to make you unclean – dirty? No he would not so why go into unclean places when you know to go into these places is a direct violation of him Good God?

Would God – Good God send you to war with another man knowing full well that killing is a sin – murder? No he would not so why do we war and fight amongst nations and each other?

Would God – Good God knowing and unknowingly take life from you when he gave you good and true life?

None of this God – Good God will do so why do we make him out to be a monster?

Like I've said, a solid foundation that is based on truth, honesty, cleanliness and goodness is key because this foundation is true and it cannot be broken. Yes I have a yoyo relationship with Good God hence these books but I need this yoyo relationship to stop. It does not become me nor does it become him.

Evil should not find its way between me and him.

Evil should not find us or come between us period; hence I need a good and solid foundation with him all around and if he cannot give me this then he Good God is not the right god and or one for me.

Good should not have to struggle at the hands of evil.

Good should not have to suffer because of evil. Nor should we live in dirty places and compounds because of evil – wicked and evil people that seek to control and destroy it all.

Good life is about fairness and justice and if you cannot have this in life then you have nothing. He Good God have to and must realize this. By him keeping his people around sinful and wicked people as well as in wicked lands that kill, he is contributing to the dirtiness of us (his people). Meaning he's causing us to sin hence committing a wilful sin.

You cannot say and or as God you cannot say the one to save humanity must live clean when the surroundings of earth is not clean but sinful – unclean – dirty. If you go into a dirty land and or place, you too will become dirty hence I have to question Good God integrity at times.

I know he wants to save his people but in truth things should have never gotten this far. You cannot say you love us so but yet leave us to die.

You cannot say you love us so and leave us in financial ruin – slavery.

You cannot say you love us so and leave us with severe health woes.

You cannot say you love us so and have no good foundation with your children – people.

You cannot say you love us so and have no good land and lands to put us in.

You cannot say you love us so and have no good family values.

You cannot say you love us so and continue to let us sin and live in sin. Come on now.

A good and strong foundation as well as good family values is essential in life and without these qualities what are we?

I've said every child need a mother and father and will forever say this but at times things don't work out this way. We can say it's the card we are dealt but no one is dealt cards in life.

Some of us choose to fight wars for our country. Is it right?

No because the law of God according to man is THOU SHALT NOT KILL.

Is this a true law of God?

Yes it is. This law is not just physical but spiritual as well. Goodness is governed by the THOU SHALT NOT KILL LAW but EVIL IS NOT GOVERNED BY IT. Evil must kill hence evil kills daily.

Evil send your child on the battlefield to be slaughtered like pigs.

Evil build guns and ammunition to kill not just the enemy but each other.

Evil design pesticides, germicides and herbicides to kill the plant life and trees including waterways of this earth.

Evil preach and teach lies and tell you it's good food whilst watching you sin and go further into hell to burn.

Evil do all that is evil for you to break away from God – Good God.

All this and more evil does but yet he Good God have not lead us to the place he needs us to be so that we can permanently break away from evil.

He Good God knows that good does not need evil.

He knows the implication of evil but yet he makes us continue to live amongst evil and this is wrong on his part.

You cannot say you are God and leave your children to die like I've said. This is wrong on his part hence he is not true and good to his word.

No one likes pain and suffering.

No one likes trials and tribulations.

No one likes heartache and pain.

No one likes stress and problems. I certainly don't, hence I try my best to avoid stress but can't. I have kids and family members that have issues.

It's like these young of today do not know the value of life. They care not about life. Some say they are going to die anyway but the death of flesh is truly not the death of life. The spirit is just breaking away from its host which is the flesh. The spirit is life all around because it is energy and this energy can and will die depending on the life you live on earth – the physical realm.

The spirit is your good or evil will.

Your good or evil genes.

Your good or evil you.

Your beautiful and or ugly you.

Your beautiful and or ugly home.

Your clean and or dirty you.

All this and more is your spirit. Your flesh is not capable of sin; your spirit is (capable of sin) because your spirit is your thought and senses. Allelujah

It is your jealousy

Your pride

Education

Family

Sight

Good and bad life and more.

We are governed by the spirit hence the spirit is hard to control nor can it be controlled because the spirit answers to a higher being and can be controlled by that higher being.

No one is in control of their destiny because none of us know what our true destiny is. Hence none of us can break away from the spirit without the flesh dying. This was not the way things were originally but because negative energy came into play it is this way for now. Yes some might say we are experiments and we are being tested but I say unto you, this is untrue. TO TEST THE SPIRIT WITH EVIL WOULD BE INFINITELY AND INDEFINITELY WRONG AND SINFUL ON GOOD GOD'S PART.

You cannot allow people to feel pain at the hands of evil because life isn't about dirty it's about clean – cleanliness.

I cannot walk on the pathway of God – Good God then go on the pathway of evil and when it does not suit me I hurry back over to the pathway of God – Good God. It simply cannot work nor will it work because you are taking God – Good God for a fool.

Right will always be right and wrong will always be wrong. Like I've said, we are the ones to do wrong and expect to get right for the wrongs that we do. We want to ignore the consequences of sin all the time whilst enjoying our evil life and this cannot be.

A good foundation knows not evil hence this foundation that I now build with Good God can never ever decay because it is good and true and of my good, true and clean good will.

Goodness don't worry about death because goodness cannot die but evil dies. Evil must die because this is a part of the laws of life. When you sin you die and you cannot get around this law. Not even God – Good God can get around this law because he too is governed by the law and laws of life and death. If he do wrong then he too must die like the ordinary man.

He cannot say he's an exception to the law because he made them. There are not exceptions here hence he too must live and be clean at all times.

Yes life may have no meaning to you because of your heartache and struggles but the heartache and struggles we face Good God did not put us in it. No, that's not true because he will put you in places for you to learn and know and or see how truthful lies can be. I've experienced this first hand hence I know how truthful lies can be. I know the lie that was told to Eve (Evening) and how truthful it was hence I can tell you about it. We lie for whatever reason and in different seasons hence we are the ones to sin. Our lies take us to hell for us to die hence we are to break away from all that is evil.

No one that is unclean can or will stand before Good God because he Good God does not associate with dirty – unclean. If you are unclean you must go down to hell for sentencing.

If you are a worker of iniquity you must go down to hell for sentencing.

If you are a murderer that kills for money and or without remorse you must go down to hell for sentencing.

If you've given your life over to death, you must go down to hell for sentencing.

If you are abusive to your parents and do all manner of evil to them you must go down to hell for sentencing.

If you constantly steal (take what does not belong to you) you must go down to hell for sentencing.

IF YOU BEAT YOUR WIFE, WOO NELLY YOU MUST GO TO HELL AND BURN FOR INDEFINITE LIFETIMES. YOU WILL NOT BE SENTENCED BECAUSE TO BEAT YOUR WIFE IS AUTOMATIC DEATH. It is forbidden for a man to beat his wife and children without just cause. And forget it, there is no just cause for a man to beat his wife.

And no it's not because I am a woman BUT IT IS THE LAW OF GOD – GOOD GOD. To beat a woman and mistreat her is DISRESPECT NOT ONLY TO HER BUT TO GOOD GOD ALSO. HE GOOD GOD IS FEMALE IN THE PHYSICAL WORLD AND MALE IN THE SPIRITUAL REALM HENCE THE MALE'S XY GENES.

Forget it about the cheating and or affair. You the husband is forbidden to hit your wife and or mate. The man and or woman that was erred is the one to lay out punishment and or beat your wife because she (your wife and or mate) has and have violated another woman's/man's home.

No one can add to or take away from the law and laws of Good God.

We are to know his law and laws so that when justice is being handed out on earth we are fair and just in our dealings.

So once again, build good, strong, truthful, honest, clean and lasting foundations with Good God.

Michelle Jean

Whatever your mansion look like make sure you have a good and strong foundation. Your beauty is your beauty as seen in the pictures above.

As with you in life you need a good foundation to build and it's the same with Good God, hence you must build wisely and truthfully.

Michelle Jean

I am but a spectator

I am but a lonely soul

I am dried up

Dried out

A prune

Stale fruit

I am a recluse

A lonely fish swimming in the ocean

I am private

Truly love privacy

I run from evil

Try all to hide from it (evil)

I want nothing to do with evil hence evil should want nothing to do with me.

I am fair

I am strong

I am weak

Disabled

Dumb

I am nature

I wither

Fade

Change with the seasons depending on if it is hot or cold.

I am a delicate flower

A rose

A fruit

Tomato

I am me

But you can't be me

I am fine

Divine

I am Michelle Jean

Michelle Jean

Through the looking glass I look

I stand at your window

Peer in

Look at you

I hope and yearn for you

Wonder what it's like to truly love you

I am but woman

I catch fade

Feelings

I have wants and desires

Needs

But on this day I look but you don't see me.

You can't see me because I am dressed in raggedy clothes

My hair is nappy and unkept

It sticks up

Flies in different directions

My shoes are cheap and not of the expensive kind

My pants have holes in them – well sewn up

My face is natural no makeup have I

Hence the blemished look well the blemishes on my face

I wear skirts

Long flowing skirts

Dresses too

Do I care to be on the best dressed list?

Hell no because I am me.

I am boring

Sometimes funny

Hey I don't even wear lipstick

Nor do I wear nail polish

Am I fake?

Hell no

The boobs are real and yes I like to flaunt them too.

Do I like bras?

No, but I can't let my jackfruits sag in public.

Got to keep them up

Let them be on display

Oh yes that's me and my assets

My girls

Play toy

Am I weird?

No, just a bit crazy because I've changed the tone of this book and I truly don't know why.

Yes with boredom comes laughter.

The mood swings

Caveman dwelling

Yes the lonely days come

Who wouldn't be if you are in a yoyo relationship with God – Good God?

It's not like you can do all that you want to do.

You are restricted

Lonely

Bored.

You look to him for release and guidance but no guidance and release comes.

You see and know where you want to be but you are stuck in this ho-hum and glum place. Your spirit cries out but it is shut up – shut down. So you make another B line of wanting to escape this spiritual dungeon – prison.

Yes jailbreak, jailbreak.

Damn there's no escape.

The warden is at the end of the hall so you have to turn around and go back to your cell.

Yes you try to escape again

It's another day and you seek your freedom.

You run here

Damn you're shut down again.

You find a different street

A different avenue

Here we go again

Yes the warden is there

He knows all your escape routes

And he shuts you down

Yes God – Good God is the warden hence good luck in trying to escape him without a good and clean key.

Yes the roads to live is sometimes wavy but you have to make your own straight path despite the curves.

Hills and valleys do come in the way. Yes some of us fall off the path but it's up to us to get back on.

We are who we are.

We are jealous human beings at times.

We are a little bit crazy – cray cray

Yes life was meant to be peaceful and smooth but how can it be when all this negativity surrounds us?

Control us

Destroy our lives.

Yes I'm at your window looking in

I am deep in thought

Homeless

Hopeful

I am sickly

Distraught

Shameless

I am your bag lady

Your street walker

Prostitute

I am your baby mama

Sister

Brother

Wife

Play thing

I am your bed

Your car

Joyful ride

Joyful noise

I am the other woman

Other man

Your business man

Business woman

Politician

I am not your church

Don't need lies

Idols

Infinitely and indefinitely don't need your gods.

I am stable

Unstable

I am a thinker

Have deep thoughts

I am your inventor

Stalker

Night Stalker

Day walker

I am your book that you can read

I am your chocolate

Good food

Your airplane that flies

I am your good drug

Hard drugs because I can be tough

A real bitch at times

I am playful but how I play is not dependant on you.

My play is my play

Hence my fun and playful days.

I am your XXX video

No scrap that

No include it because I can be perverse depending on the sexual nature of my mind – spirit.

I am your toy

Your glee

Your plantain

Green and ripe banana

I am your Jackfruit

Millie Mango

Watermelon

I am our honey dew

Mountain grown coffee

I am your herbs and spices

Neatly kept and well kept garden

I am your rose

Your candle

The water that bathes you

But with all that said

I am the one looking in your window

You can't see me but I can see you

To you I am not there

I am but a stranger

I cannot be your flower

Because I am big and bold

Chubby

Fat

I have nappy hair

Short

Gray

I am old

Not pretty

I am brown skin

Black skin

Dark skin

I am black and beautiful

Proud of my black lineage

Damn proud to be exact

I hold my head up in blackness because BLACK AM I AND I AM PROUD.

Proud of my black history

Proud of my black god

Proud to be black all around

Proud of my good black doctors

Good black nurses

Good black teachers

Good black people

Good black inventors

Good black man

Good black woman

Good black child

Good black children

Yes I'm black

Black am I because I fall under the banner of black and that is good life all around.

Yes I am black

I am not good for you – some of you because you made it so

I am not a part of your social plan because to you black is not beautiful BUT YET YOU WANT TO LOOK LIKE ME

You want to be tanned like me

Black like me

You want my hair but can't get it

Your genes is my genes hence you can't be black like me

You know not truth

The truth of your history

My history

Origins

You know not God – Good God hence you can't be black like me

Yes I am black and I am proud but with all that said you can't see me.

I am the one looking in your window

I am the one broken

Like a broken glass

Cup

Chandelier

I am the one holding the coffee and donut but you cannot accept it because I look like the Black Raggedy Anne.

I am not black like you nor are you black.

My colour is not perfect nor is it right for you.

My hair is not perfect nor is it right for you.

My look is not right for you because I am not white like you nor am I black like you.

I am not Asian like you

Nor will I be Babylonian like you.

I am not right in your world hence I am the one looking in your window.

Wondering

Pondering

Wishing

Yearning not to be like you.

I am me

Perfect in my world

Perfect in my thought hence I am not like YOU

I am not self made but made in truth by God – Good God.

I am rich in thought

In all that I do

I am spiritual and physical

Divine but not divine like you.

Your divinity is your divinity hence our god is not the same.

I truly have life and you have death hence I am not like you and will never be like you. Don't want to be either hence I am the one standing at your window and looking in.

I shake my head and walk away with coffee and donut in hand.

In all that I see, I do not want to know you because what I see is not what I need. You are the ungrateful and sinful one. You are not perfect hence I walk away from sin and this sinful world – all sinful things.

Your mountain is not my mountain

Your world is not my world

Your life is not my life

So as I turn to leave

Leave

I see no humanity in you

Just lies

Games played by you to keep the world and society satisfied.

I see the lies

The game

The ego

The wolf's clothing

The deceit

Satan's world coming out of you and in you.

You are a grey goose of lies

Hence you are grey but not grey like me.

Your hair is not nappy like mine hence you cannot be fine

Cannot be truthful and of the truth

You're not black like me hence you know not what truth and honour is

You love to lie hence you live in lies

Pay for dates

Flakes

Lies

You are a well dressed pimp

Like onto a high end and or class prostitute

You live for lies

Devotion

Fake ass beauty

Tricks not the cereal though

You are a player that has caught fade because you don't know when to stop even with your dried up libido.

Fake fake fake

All that is about you is fake

Self hate

Narcissistically done

Egotistical

Demonic

Fruity

Ah I am back on my mountain again

I am at peace

True peace

All is tranquil until I let loose again.

Loneliness is good at times but with Good God you must stay truly clean.

Yes you can vent

Pop off

Get off

But in truth, real truth, it's good to be Black

Black and good

Yes I am right in thought

Words

Life but it could be better

Don't like the sick days

Oh man I so don't like them.

Yes I am rich

Truly rich in God – Good God because I write for him.

Just poor financially but yet super rich financially because he chose me

I am free but yet enslaved

Tied

Can't do what I truly want to do

I am fine

A true friend to him because I get to vent to him in this way and I am hoping he truly likes it.

Yes I am free

I am black

Black like me

As black as I want to be

I am wealthy

No so healthy

BUT I AM BLACK AND THAT'S HOW I NEED MY LIFE TO BE.

I AM A PROUD BLACK WOMAN AND NO ONE IS AS PROUD AS ME.

I look to my black history

My black truth

My black pride because black is in me and it's good to be black all around.

I have nappy hair that stands up like an antenna when I sleep. Yes my nappy hair is my communication tool.

Ah yes I am blessed to have nappy hair once again.

Don't need the chemical and or pre treated look.

Don't need another person's nasty human hair on my head because I am proud to be black and more than infinitely and indefinitely proud of my true communication tool – my nappy and happy hair.

I can plat it

Twist it

Leave it poufy and fluffy

I can roll it like a sliff

Leave it natural like Buddha

Well Buddha took our look because Buddha be black – a Black African. We all know where the Chinese race came from hence they are at the base of the mountain.

Yes it's perfect and wonderful to be black – TRUE BLACK – NATURAL BLACK.

I am black and you're not black and wonderful like me.

I am perfect because to be black means to be like God – Good God.

Yes I am black and proud of me.

I am full black hence the nappy hair and black genes in me.

I am of creation and creation is of me.

I am perfect for God and Good God is perfect for me because he is black too. Fall under the banner of black like me.

He is life and life is in me.

Yes he created me and set me in time for a time hence time in time.

He is the key to life – everlasting life.

He's the key to all the universes within time – set in time.

Ah it's good to know God – Good God hence one day we all can and will say well done you received me and did good and well by me.

Michelle Jean

It's May 04, 2014 and this book is done but for me it is not done because I had this confusing dream this morning.

I dreamt Kenya this morning and I as I close this book with Kenya, I pray that he Good God protect Kenya and the people of Kenya from everlasting unto everlasting in goodness and in truth because of goodness – true goodness bestowed upon me by a Kenyan family. I cannot forsake Kenya because when I needed a home – roof over my head I was given this help. So because of true goodness and true good will Good God I come to you for peace, true peace and ask that you remember the land and people due to kindness and goodness to me and my family. You are my glory and truth and what I saw in my vision I truly do not comprehend nor understand. Hence you are my Ark of Glory and Truth. You are my everlasting unto everlasting and as I come to you in truth for the Ark of Covenant – land and people let your glory flourish and radiate throughout the universe and universes including your good lands and people of earth. As I look at beauty, your beautiful people I pray them to keep in goodness and truth.

This morning I dreamt clothing and colours such as these people are wearing but the patterns of the clothing – I call it clothing was confusing. It was as if pure confusion was all around and I could not make sense of the pattern.

The sword on the flag I remember but I cannot tell you about it. What I remember is a bagel like the one below.

I saw a knife and the knife cutting the bagel in half. I did not see a person cutting the bagel. All I saw was the bagel being cut in half and I woke up out of my sleep.

In truth Good God I truly do not know what this dream means. I am seeing dry dreams now and they are confusing and hard to decipher because they are dreams within a dream.

I have an idea about the dream in regards to dividing of north from south and or the division from other African lands but I am not sure and I do not want to speculate on this lest I be wrong. I know for a fact that Kenya is an old nation and country that has been around from before the conception of man because that land holds the spear of death and your ark. The spear that is on the flag of their nation is the spear that kills death; more specifically the demons of hell. Meaning in the spiritual realm once the demon has been separated from its spiritual host, this spear, the spear of Kenya kills demons in the spiritual realm.

Good God I do not know what the cutting of the bagel means because the bagel was cut in half – separated.

I do not know if devastation is going to be on the land. If destruction and or devastation in the form of earthquakes, political unrest, financial unrest, health woes is due to come for this country, I ask in goodness and truth to squash it, send all unrest and destruction back to where it came from and do not let anything happen to this country and people.

Goodness was bestowed to me and my family by a Kenyan family and it is in goodness and in truth I am begging (asking) for Kenya and the people of Kenya. Please keep this country safe because goodness was done unto me hence goodness was bestowed and done unto you.

Good God I have to plea with you for the goodness of this country. You gave me truth Good God and I have to be truthful to you and remember kindness. So because of kindness and truth Kenya must be saved. It is my true and good will hence true and good will of you.

Michelle Jean

OTHER BOOKS BY MICHELLE JEAN

Blackman Redemption – The Fall of Michelle Jean
Blackman Redemption – After the Fall Apology
Blackman Redemption – World Cry – Christine Lewis
Blackman Redemption
Blackman Redemption – The Rise and Fall of Jamaica
Blackman Redemption – The War of Israel
Blackman Redemption – The Way I Speak to God
Blackman Redemption – A Little Talk With Man
Blackman Redemption – The Den of Thieves
Blackman Redemption – The Death of Jamaica
Blackman Redemption – Happy Mother's Day
Blackman Redemption – The Death of Faith
Blackman Redemption – The War of Religion
Blackman Redemption – The Death of Russia
Blackman Redemption – The Truth
Blackman Redemption – Spiritual War

The New Book of Life
The New Book of Life – A Cry For The Children
The New Book of Life – Judgement
The New Book of Life – Love Bound
The New Book of Life – Me
The New Book of Life – Life

Just One of Those Days
Book Two – Just One of Those Days
Just One of Those Days – Book Three The Way I Feel
Just One of Those Days – Book Four

The Days I Am Weak
Crazy Thoughts – My Book of Sin
Broken
Ode to Mr. Dean Fraser

A Little Little Talk
A Little Little Talk – Book Two

Prayers
My Collective
A Little Talk/A Time For Fun and Play

Simple Poems
Behind The Scars
Songs of Praise And Love

Love Bound
Love Bound – Book Two

Dedication Unto My Kids
More Talk
Saving America From A Woman's Perspective
My Collective the Other Side of Me
My Collective the Dark Side of Me
A Blessed Day
Lose To Win
My Doubtful Days – Book One

My Little Talk With God
My Little Talk With God – Book Two

A Different Mood and World – Thinking

My Nagging Day
My Nagging Day – Book Two

Friday September 13, 2013
My True Love
It Would Be You
My Day

A Little Advice – Talk
1313, 2032, 2132 – The End of Man
Tata

MICHELLE'S BOOK BLOG – BOOKS 1 – 16

My Problem Day
A Better Way
Stay – Adultery and the Weight of Sin – Cleanliness Message

Let's Talk